IMAGES
of England

AROUND GARFORTH

IMAGES
of England

AROUND GARFORTH

Garforth Historical Society

TEMPUS

Church Lane with the wall of the churchyard on the right. The cottages on the left no longer stand, having made way for an entrance into the Oak Estate.

Frontispiece:
Station Fields, looking towards the station. St Benedict's school and playing fields (left) and Marlowe Court (right) stand here today.

First published 2002
Copyright © Garforth Historical Society, 2002

Tempus Publishing Limited
The Mill, Brimscombe Port,
Stroud, Gloucestershire, GL5 2QG

ISBN 0 7524 2614 1

Typesetting and origination by
Tempus Publishing Limited
Printed in Great Britain by
Midway Colour Print, Wiltshire

Contents

Acknowledgements   6

Introduction   7

1. Pits and Coal   9

2. Other Occupations   15

3. Churches and Chapels   31

4. Education   45

5. Main Street   55

6. Transport   73

7. People   85

8. Buildings   95

9. General Views   119

Acknowledgements

Thanks must go to the members of the Garforth Historical Society, especially Margaret Benn, Roger Davies and Ron Sudderdean, for the production of this publication.

Some factual details were extracted from the Society's book, *A Short History of Garforth*, (currently in print) and from *Mediaeval Garforth*, by John I. Rushton, to whom the Society is indebted.

Many people have lent us photographs over the last twenty-five years; we thank them here and apologize to anyone whose name has been omitted in error.

Dennis Astin, John Barber, Harold Bramley, Marjorie Brown, Paul Stuart Clark, Barry Dodsworth, Winnie Gaythorpe, Gladys Gisburn, Mr Gray, Mr and Mrs Harry Goodall, Mrs Griffin, Frank Holroyd, Graham Hudson, Pat Howson, W. and I. Jacob, Gladys Maltby, Dennis Riley, Mrs L. Ryder, Tom Pickering, Walter Pickles, Mary Preston, Margaret Simpson, Mrs Stocks, Mrs Margaret Surrey, Gerry Symes, Dorothy and Don Tillotson, Derek and Pat Toes, Jack Waters, Mrs B. Ward, Vera Willis, Janet Yelland.

Introduction

Though there is little visible evidence, Garforth has a long history. In 1998 preparations for a housing development at the boundary of East Garforth and Sturton Grange revealed a Romano-British settlement with potsherds of the shiny red Samian ware, evidence of a Roman stone quarry and a coin of Emperor Commodius, who reigned in AD 180.

The entry in Domesday Book, initiated by William the Conqueror in 1086, records that Gereford was part of the estate of Ilbert de Laci, who was based at Pontefract, and was one of the 200 manors in the Barony of Pontefract. The entry shows the population as being four villagers' families and one cottager only, yet there is a church and a priest which suggests it had been larger. Indeed, Domesday gives the value of the vill in 1086 as 30s, though it adds that it had been 60s in the time of Edward the Confessor, which also suggests that the population had fallen.

The manor of Church Garforth came about when Ilbert de Laci gave land to the abbey of St Mary at York in 1089. West Garforth was a separate manor on land given by the de Lacis to the Stapletons of Swillington. A charter of 1180 refers to Robert of Swillington having a mill between Swillington and Garforth which evidence suggests was at Garforth Bridge, powered by the water of Sheffield Beck (which has nothing to do with Sheffield but is a corruption of Sheep Field).

A poll tax levied in 1380 by Richard II recorded forty-nine people over the age of fifteen who were eligible for tax, excluding clerics and beggars. The wealthiest person is shown as Johannes de Garforth. Tax evasion is nothing new and the number of tax payers does not necessarily give a correct number of the population. Many householders concealed elderly relatives and older children.

At this time Garforth was purely agricultural but the Gascoigne family were to have a major influence in the development of Garforth. They are believed to be descended from a Saxon noble, Ailrichus. Banished from the country, the family is said to have settled in Gascony, returning with William the Conqueror to live in Harewood and Gawthorpe. It was here that Sir William Gascoigne was born in 1350. His younger brother, Nicholas Gascoigne, founded the Parlington and Barnbow branch of the family. He settled at Lazencroft in 1391 and also owned some land in Church Garforth and West Garforth. Thomas, Lord Wentworth, sold Parlington Hall to John Gascoigne in 1545. It was from here that the Gascoignes purchased the manor of West Garforth from Robert Hemsworth, including 200 acres and a windmill, in 1566. In 1625 all manors were mortgaged to provide Charles I with revenue, but in 1677 Ledston and

Garforth were held in trust for Sir Thomas Gascoigne of Barnbow and the family became lords of the manor of Garforth.

There is an early reference to coal mining in 1582 when Richard Gascoigne of Lazencroft was prosecuted for mining coal, but he was able to prove that the pit was on his own manor at Shippen, nearby. By the sixteenth century coal mining was quite extensive and Sir John Gascoigne had workings in Barnbow, Lazencroft and Whinmoor, mostly worked from outcrops, shallow pits and short levels. It was between 1830 and 1840, when the population of Garforth was 782, that the Gascoignes sank their first pit shaft in Garforth. The pits were named after the family. Isabella opened in 1833. Shortly after a second pit was named after Elizabeth. Sisters pit was sunk in 1843 and Trench pit in Ninelands Lane, sunk in 1899, was named after Isabella's husband who changed his name to Gascoigne on his marriage. These collieries were a major source of employment in Garforth, no longer purely agricultural. Just before the Great War the output from Garforth pits rose to 440,000 tons a year.

Not only did the Gascoignes provide employment, however. In 1737 Sir Edward Gascoigne agreed to provide land in the village that would produce an income of 50s a year towards maintaining a schoolmaster. In 1843 the Gascoigne sisters built the Colliery School at East Garforth for the miners' children. Such was the regard for the Gascoignes as employers that in 1865, when miners went on strike throughout the district, Garforth miners did not take part and the Gascoignes showed their appreciation by building a Working Men's Club. The prosperity did not continue and in 1919 Colonel Gascoigne sold his mining interests. Sisters pit was worked out in 1922 and Isabella in 1925, when pumps were stopped and the workings flooded. At the latter pit alone 392 men lost their jobs. There is little to remind us of the colliery village as the pits have gone completely, with the exception of a tree-covered spoil heap behind a supermarket and a brick engine house in the yard of a block manufacturers. The Miners' Welfare Hall is now the Community Centre, only the Miners' Arms serves to recall our past industry.

Administratively, Garforth in medieval times had a Manor Court, first under Ilbert de Laci, then the Earl of Lancaster and eventually the Gascoignes. Changes at the end of the eighteenth century meant that Garforth acquired a parish council under Tadcaster Rural Council. After the Local Government Act of 1894, Garforth applied for urban status and, in March 1908, Garforth Urban District was created.

After the Second World War and the sharp increase in population, the demand for housing meant that developers sought green-field sites. Houses sprang up on the eastern side of Garforth with Grange estate, Ninelands estate, the Meadows and, more recently, at East Garforth. With the abolition of the Urban District Council in 1974, Garforth lost control of its affairs and is administered by Leeds Metropolitan Council, to become just part of the ever-growing urban sprawl.

As a Historical Society it is our task to inform future citizens of their heritage. The past must not be forgotten. At the same time we hope that this book will enable older Garfordians to recall their own memories of earlier times.

One
Pits and Coal

Sisters pit was just north of the present Safeway store and houses have been built on part of the site. The spoil heap, off-picture to the left, still exists covered with trees.

Isabella pit, down Ash Lane, was named after one of the Gascoigne sisters. The private 'Fly Line' ran from Sisters pit, through Isabella pit and on to Aberford coal staithes.

Reactions to attempts to improve wages and conditions caused a strike in 1919, a lock-out in 1921 and the General Strike in 1926. Office staff and the Navy were used for maintenance. After 1926 only Trench pit remained open.

Coal wagons and the generating station at Sisters pit. Electricity would be used for both ventilation and the winding gear.

A stall set up in Main Street, opposite where Greenway is now, during the 1921 strike. It sold fish cheaply. A soup kitchen was also provided and sixty-six children at the Parochial School received vouchers for meals.

Trench pit, in Ninelands Lane, was named after Col. Richard Oliver Trench who married Isabella Gascoigne and then took the name Trench-Gascoigne in order to keep the right to the estate. This pit was the last one open in Garforth. It closed in 1930.

This scene from Garforth Cliff in 1960 shows the remains of Trench pit, Archibald Johnson's works and Nightingale's transport depot – all in Ninelands Lane. The foreground railway ran from Garforth to Castleford via Kippax.

Trench pit officials and sailors brought in to protect the pit during a strike in the 1920s. From left to right, back row: S. Clark (engineer), four sailors, F. Whitaker (electrician). Middle row includes; C. Wardle (shot firer), Mrs C. Straw, C. Straw, the rest unknown. Front row: two sailors, Mr Straw Jnr, J. Wigglesworth (deputy).

13

'Through sylvan glades' on the way down the Fly Line to Aberford. In the early twentieth century many Garforth residents took a walk down the line as a regular pastime.

The ladies put on a Pierrot show for funds to support their menfolk during one of the pit strikes.

Two
Other Occupations

West Garforth Farm, owned by Mr Horner, stood on Selby Road close to the point where the footpath emerges from Goosefields – land he also farmed. The cart is loaded with their main crop, rhubarb, which was supplied to Covent Garden.

West Garforth farmhouse. The small child, just visible to the right of the doorway, is Gladys Stringer, later Mrs Maltby, whose father, Henry, was farm foreman until 1940.

Mr Stringer and his horse team. He enjoyed driving them down Main Street with their gleaming harness.

Mrs Stringer feeding poultry at West Garforth Farm. Behind her is one of the rhubarb sheds which were brought from Barnbow munitions factory after the First World War.

View across Goosefields, Ringway and the Alandales when it was just farmland. Barrowby Ridge is in the distance. Mr Henry Stringer is on pest patrol.

Manor Farm was an experimental farm and dairy unit run by Leeds University until 1928 when it was relocated at Askam Bryan.

The interior of the Dairy Unit. Girls came from places such as Skipton to learn improved methods of production. Buttermilk, 'blue milk', was sold to local children.

Experimental plots of grasses, to improve cattle feed, grown at Manor Farm.

The nearest two houses, one named Stoneleigh, were used as lodgings for dairymaids at Manor Farm. This postcard was sent to Miss Smith, Beech Farm, Addingham, and asks if she recognizes the house. Maybe she is an ex-trainee.

WILLIAM GREEN,

Builder of Grottoes, Ferneries, Rockeries & Horticultural Buildings;

ALSO CONTRACTOR FOR LANDSCAPE GARDENING,
of which, Plans and Estimates may be had on application.

W. G. will be glad to forward Catalogues of Fruit, Forest and Ornamental Trees and Roses, also for Bulbs, Seeds, &c.

THE YORKSHIRE FINE ART & INDUSTRIAL EXHIBITION,

HELD AT LEEDS ON THE 14th OF MAY, 1875,
AND OPENED BY H.R.H. THE DUKE OF EDINBURGH;
ALSO AT YORK, OPENED MAY 1879.

THE WHOLE OF THE

Plant and Floral Decorations, Cork Work, &c.

WERE SUPPLIED, DURING THE WHOLE OF THE SIX MONTHS, BY

WILLIAM GREEN,

OF THE

Nurseries, Garforth, & 44, Vicar Lane, Leeds.

Best Selected Virgin Cork, 20s. per bale; also all kinds of Peat Soil, SILVER SAND, COCOA FIBRE, &c.

AQUARIUMS, WINDOW FERNERIES, FERN CASES, GOLD AND SILVER FISH.

An 1884 advertisement. Everyone who was anyone needed a Grotto! Their shop still existed, in Vicar Lane, in the 1950s.

Green's Nurseries in Aberford Road which later became Crummock's farm and is now the site of the Catholic church.

Potato picking in fields that are now the site of the Meadows estate. Trench pit and John Barber's house, on Ninelands Spur, are in the distance.

Another of John Barber's gang, this time picking raspberries. He employed gangs from Garforth and Kippax, and some rivalry existed between them.

Drinking at harvest-time on Pickering's farmland. For many years the Pickerings were very well-respected wholesale and retail butchers.

A pig in a poke? Not quite, but Pickering's butchers raised their own animals, for slaughter, on land at Parlington. Seen here with stockman John Kennedy.

Tom Pickering's staff at their slaughterhouse behind the Main Street shop. The group includes Walter Learoyd (centre), Mrs Smith (standing behind him) and John Simpson, who is the young man at the extreme right of the picture.

A suckling pig being prepared for the Queen's Hotel, Leeds, by Pickering's staff.

This oil painting shows where, in the early twentieth century, a Mr Rickard quarried sand under Garforth Cliff for use in foundries. Full tubs ran by gravity to the railway at Ninelands and were drawn back by horse when empty.

A rare interior view of Beevers' joinery workshop in Wakefield Road. The site is now a garage, in front of the Recreation Ground.

During the First World War a railway line, seen here under construction, was quickly laid to Barnbow munitions factory. It is shown running towards Barrowby Ridge and the Leeds/Selby railway line.

Barnbow munitions factory canteen, c. 1916. Local girls were recruited and conscripted. Thirty-eight trains each day brought 16,000 workers from within a 20-mile radius. Milk for the canteen was supplied by 120 cows on the factory's own farm.

Mill buildings on Aberford Road, now the site of Beaconsfield House. Originally a flour mill, run by Grays, then a grass mill during the Second World War, it was, lastly, a depot for the local council.

George B. Marshall and Sons were local builders and brick makers. This original drain cover is at a house in Wakefield Road. Clay was extracted from the site to make some of the bricks from which the houses on the site were built.

This fine action shot shows the demolition of the chimney at Marshall's brickworks to make way for Halliday Court flats.

ESTABLISHED 1865.

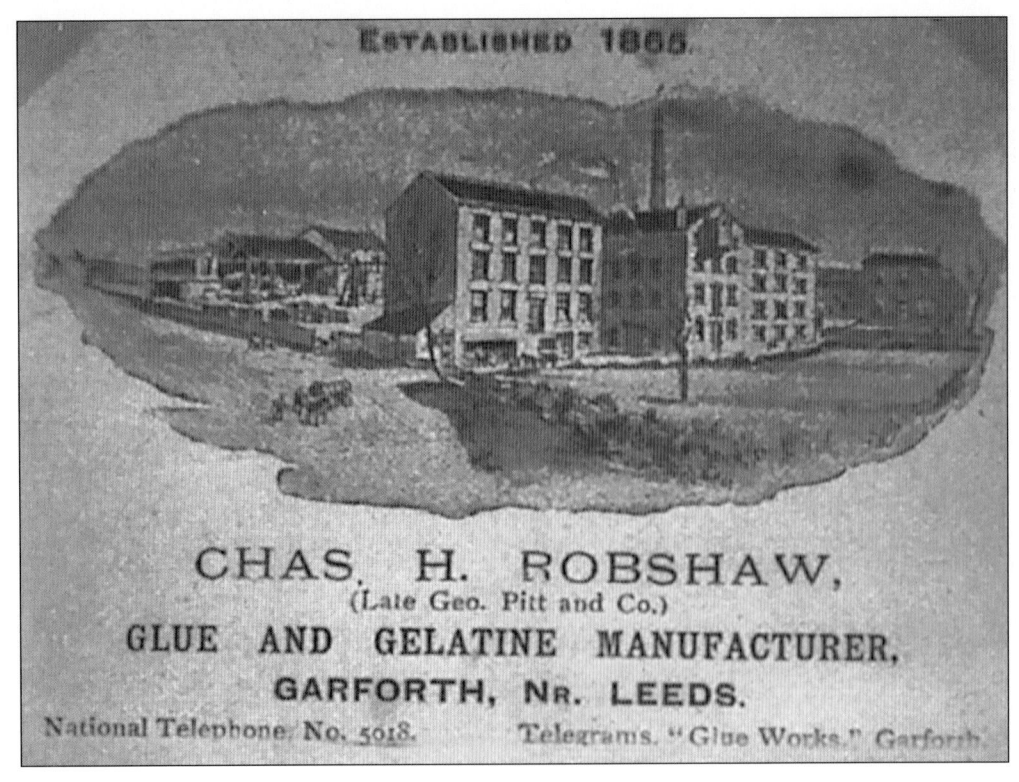

CHAS. H. ROBSHAW,
(Late Geo. Pitt and Co.)
GLUE AND GELATINE MANUFACTURER,
GARFORTH, Nr. LEEDS.

National Telephone No. 5018.　　　Telegrams. "Glue Works," Garforth.

This factory, later Naylor Pollards shirt factory, had several earlier lives, one of which can be seen here.

The Garforth Bridge shirt factory, which also made 'Pilot' overalls, is now the site of the postal sorting office. Many local girls worked here.

28

A volunteer fire brigade around 1912.

The Auxiliary Fire Service was formed before the Second World War and later became the National Fire Service. This picture includes two Greenwood brothers and a tender of 1937 vintage.

Green's of Barrowby Lane had a coal business. Seaton's and Dobson's were also coal retailers in the days when everyone had a coal fire.

An aerial view of Barwick Road with Cock Beck Bridge at the top and Manor Farm on the left. From the visible field marks it is hardly surprising that a burial cremation urn was recovered here when the road was re-aligned over the motorway.

Three
Churches and Chapels

A church is recorded in Garforth in Domesday and possesses a full list of rectors from 1249. This painting shows Garforth 'Old' church. Probably the second on the site, it was demolished in 1844. The present church was erected in 1845 with financial help from the Gascoigne sisters who rebuilt the old east window, as a folly, near the lake formed by damming Cock Beck in Parlington Hollins.

St Mary's Church, Garforth. Note the absence of clocks which were later inserted but only on three sides, as no-one lived on the Kippax side. A Mr Kirk paid for the clocks which were kept five minutes fast to allow him time to catch his train.

An interior view of St Mary's Church.

TO THE GLORIOUS MEMORY OF THE OFFICERS NON-COMMISSIONED OFFICERS AND MEN FROM GARFORTH WHO GAVE THEIR LIVES FOR THEIR COUNTRY IN THE GREAT WAR 1914 – 1919

Killed in France.
Breed John B. 2nd Lt.276/Sge.Batty.R.G.A.
Sissons Roland E. Lt.1/8 West Yorks Regt.

Died in Hospital. Kantara. Egypt.
Dobson Reginald G. Maj.M.G.C.6/W.Yorks Rgt.

Killed, or died in France.
Archer David R.L./Cpl.15/York & Lancs Regt.
Backhouse Sidney Pte.13/Durham L.Inf.
Barber James Pte. 7/K.O.Y.L.I.
Barker Frank Sergt.2/Border Regt.
Bedell Ernest Cpl.1/5 W.Yorks Regt.
Bilton Cephas Pte.1/8 W. Yorks Regt.
Breckon Robert E. L/Cpl. 6/ K.O.Y.L.I.
Brownridge Percy Pte. 3/ North'd Fus.
Brownridge Thomas A.L/Cpl.2G/F'd Co.R.E.
Burnley Herbert Pte. 15/W.Yorks Regt.
Caygill Percy Pte. 18/W.Yorks R'gt.
Cockram Richard Pte.9/D of W. Regt.
Dacre George Pte. 8/ W. Yorks Regt.
Dickinson Herbert E Pte. 7/Leices. Regt.
Dixon Robert C.L./Cpl.1/ K.O.S.B.
Freshwater Herbert Gnr.99/Bde.R.G.A.
Gee Joseph Cpl.9/ K.O.Y. L.I.
Glover Ernest Pte. 2/4 K.O.Y. L.I.
Goodall Arthur Pte 14/York & Lancs Rgt.
Gregson Harry Sergt.95/Bde R.F.A.
Hepple Leonard Pte.40/M.G.C.,R.G.A.
Hewitt Harold E.L./Cpl.9/ K.R.R.C.
Holden Leonard Dvr.245/W.B.Bde.3/R.F.A.
Howson Thomas Pte. 10/ K.O.Y. L.I.
Isherwood William E. Pte.9/D.of W. Regt.
Johnson George Sergt.2/Scots Gds.
Johnson John L/Cpl.6/Notts & Derby Rt.
Jones Edward L.P. L/Cpl.10/ W. Yorks Regt.
King John W. L/Cpl.2/Lancs.Fusiliers.
Nicholson Joe Pte. 3/Coldstream Guards.
Levitt Percy L/Cpl.10/ K.O.Y. L.I.
Oxloby Seth L/Cpl.15/Highland L.Inf.
Pickersgill Herbert Pte.14/ North'd Fus.
Quigley James Pte. 10/ K.O.Y. L.I.
Reed William Gnr. 25/Siege Batty.R.G.A.
Roberts George Spr. 44/C.C.S.R.E.
Roberts James A.S. Pte. 5/K.O.Y. L.I.
Seaton Ernest Pte. 12/Manchester Regt.
Simpson Charles Pte. 2/Coldstream Gds.
Sissons G. Reginald Cpl.9/ W. Yorks Regt.
Smith Sidney M. Pte. 10/ K.O.Y. L.I.
Smith Walter E. Cpl.9/ K.R.R.C.
Taylor Richard A. Pte. 3/ K.O.Y. L.I.
Teale Nathan Pte. 2/Coldstream Guards
Teale Richard T.L. Pte 5/ North'd. Fus.
Tillotson William Pte. 6/ Yorks. Regt.
Waites John H. Pte. 7/ K.O.Y. L.I.
Watts Thomas Cpl. 193/Inf. Labour Coy.
Wilson William F. Spr. 2/1 London R.E.

Died in Hospital. England.
Balme John E. Pte. 15/ W. Yorks Regt.
Birch Thomas Pte. 21/ W. Yorks Regt.
Dickinson Thomas Pte. 10/ K.O.Y. L.I.
Hebden John Tpr.2/Cav.Div.R.Scots Greys
Lincoln Ernest Pte. 5/ K.O.Y. L.I.
Simpson Charles I? Pte.R.T.E.B.Div.R.E.
Smithson Henry Sergt.83/F'd Amb.R.A.M.C.

Died in Hospital. Egypt.
Booth Ernest Pte. 6/ York & Lancs Regt.
Fryer Harry Pte. 33/ F'd Amb. R.A.M.C.

This tablet is erected by Colonel Gascoigne D.S.O.
"LEST WE FORGET."

Several family names on this commemorative plaque in St Mary's Church are still well known in Garforth today.

1939 – 1945
KILLED OR DIED ON ACTIVE SERVICE

MAURICE BARKER	ARTHUR STANLEY LORRIMAN
FRANK BLEASBY	STANLEY NAYLOR
HORACE CAPPER	JOHN ROBERT PRENTICE
SYDNEY CHAPPEL	GEORGE PRENTICE
THOMAS CRAVEN	BERNARD RICHARDSON
HARRY GRAY	WILLIAM ROBINSON
HAROLD HEALAS	ALEC SIMPSON
WALTER HORNER	NORMAN SIMPSON
BERNARD JACKSON	ERIC ELSTON SMITH
JACK LAMBERT	COLIN SUNDERLAND
REGINALD LEAROYD	JEFFREY ANDREW WALKER

WILLIAM WHEATLEY
1951   GORDON R LAND

The Roll of Honour of the Second World War in St Mary's Church.

Garforth Church Choir in the days when Mr Hammerton was the rector.

A view of the church from Green Lane across Atkinson's farm. Notice one of the three clocks just above Rose Villa, which was demolished to build Rose Court.

Garforth had a very active Salvation Army unit which included this fine band. They would play at Town End every Sunday.

The Salvation Army Citadel was in Coupland Road, just visible on the right-hand side of this picture.

Salvation Army Harvest Festival.

Garforth Salvationists, from left to right: John Higgins, Philip Mallison, Bandmaster Tommy Kilburn, Albert Kilburn (Tommy's son), Lt Thornton, Gilbert Mallison, unknown lady officer, and children Molly Mallison (later Mrs Richardson) and her sister Peggy.

The Primitive Methodist Chapel in Chapel Lane. This building is now the home of La Pointe School of Dance.

A memorial stone at the Salem Methodist Chapel in Wakefield Road.

The Salem Methodist Chapel in earlier times.

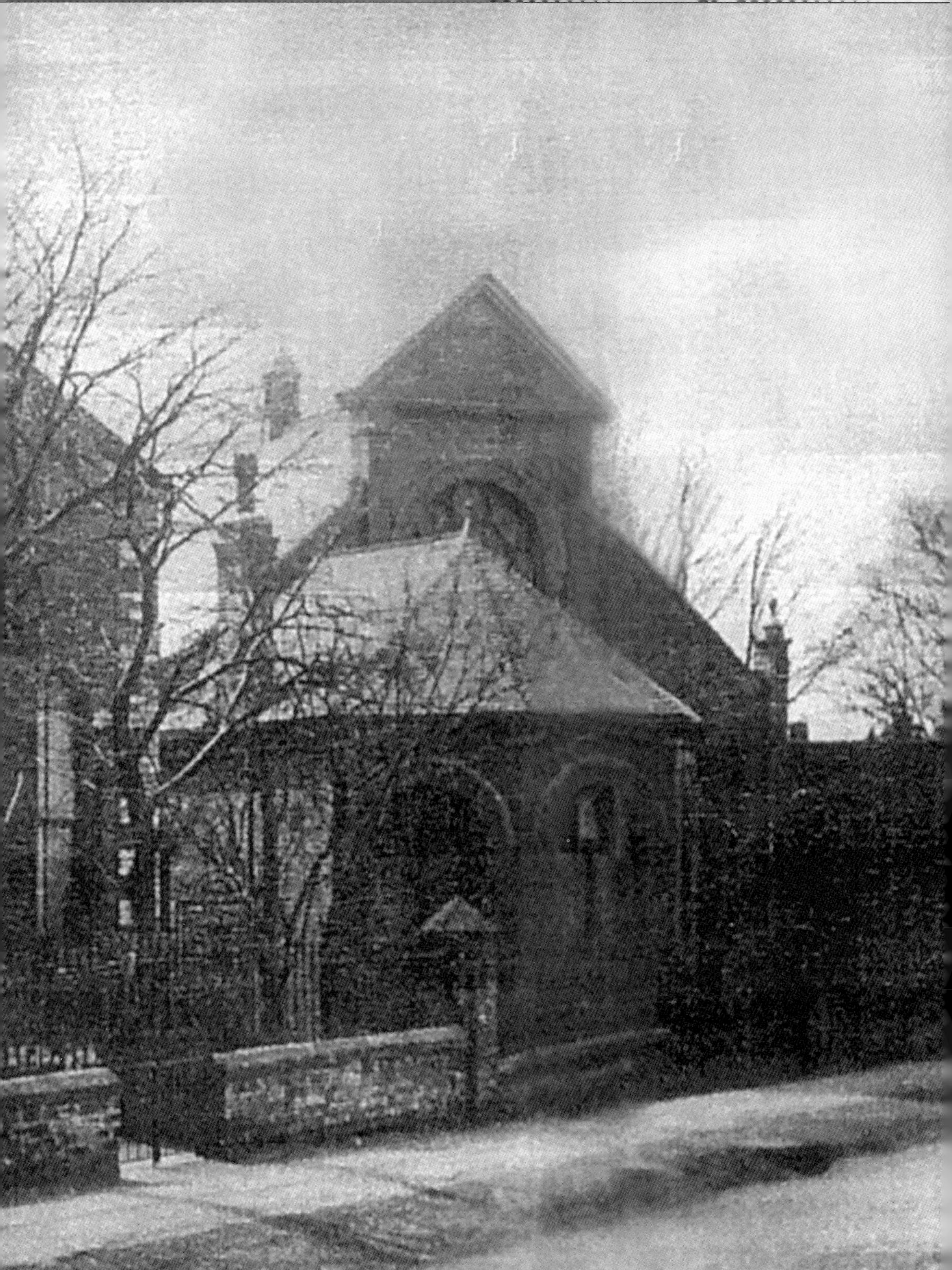

Salem Chapel, remarkably little changed from the previous picture, in its new role as the Evangelical Church.

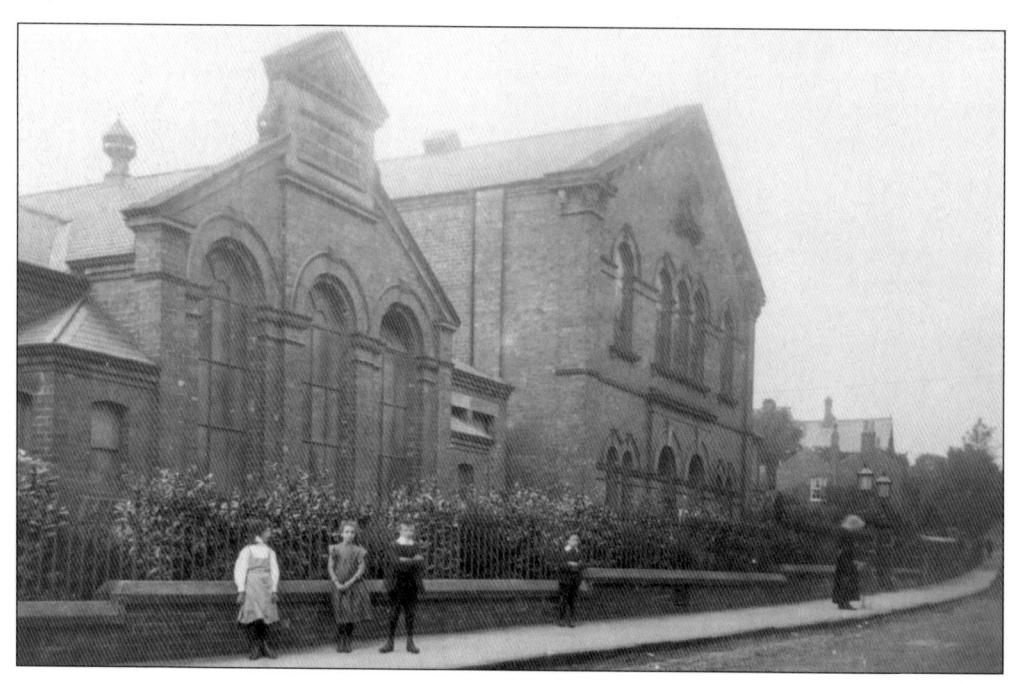

The Wesleyan Chapel in Church Lane, complete with iron railings later removed in the Second World War. This building now serves all Methodist worshippers in Garforth.

GARFORTH & KIPPAX
WESLEYAN MAGAZINE.

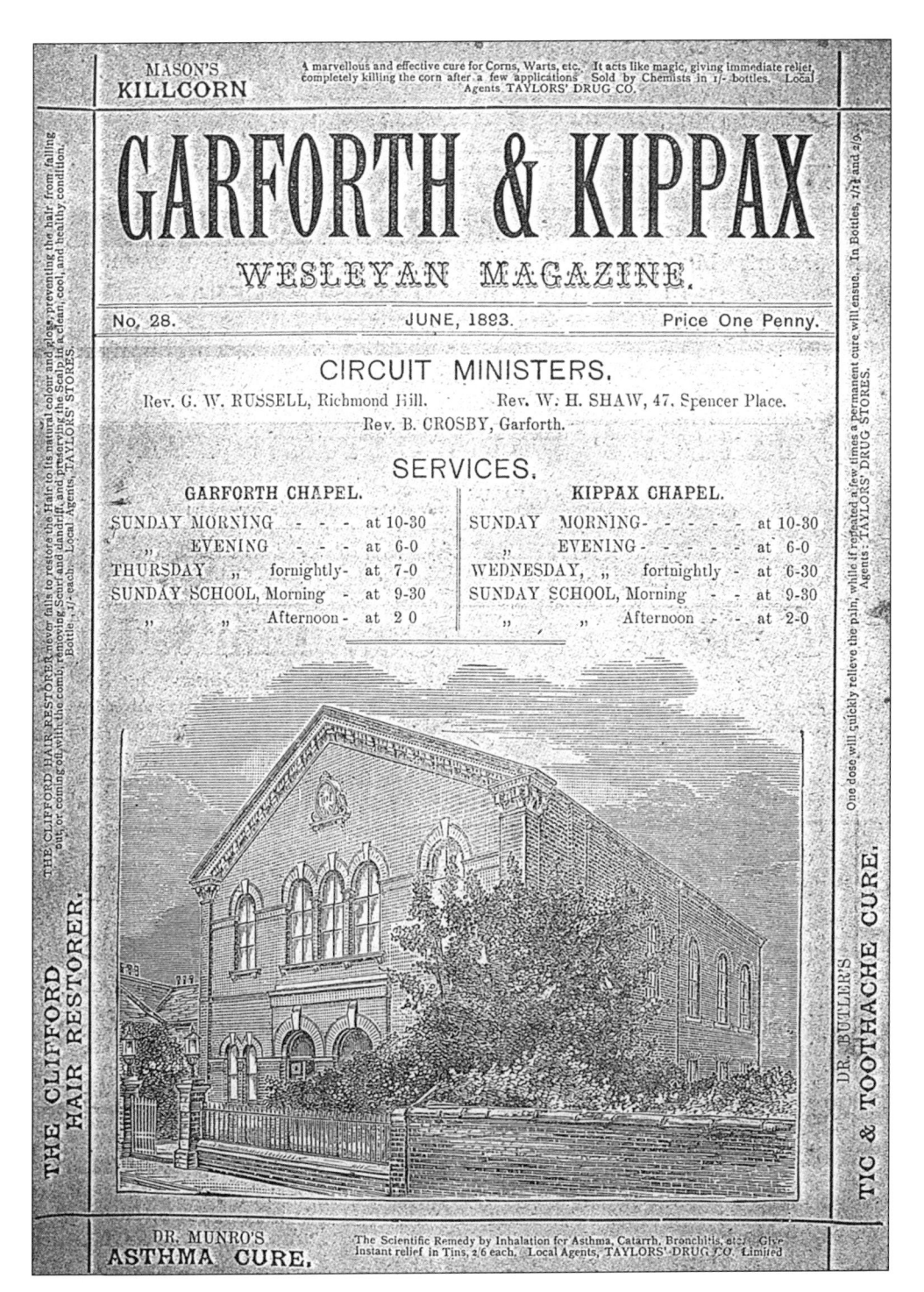

No. 28.   JUNE, 1893.   Price One Penny.

CIRCUIT MINISTERS.

Rev. G. W. RUSSELL, Richmond Hill.   Rev. W. H. SHAW, 47, Spencer Place.
Rev. B. CROSBY, Garforth.

SERVICES.

GARFORTH CHAPEL.		KIPPAX CHAPEL.	
SUNDAY MORNING	at 10-30	SUNDAY MORNING	at 10-30
,, EVENING	at 6-0	,, EVENING	at 6-0
THURSDAY ,, fortnightly	at 7-0	WEDNESDAY ,, fortnightly	at 6-30
SUNDAY SCHOOL, Morning	at 9-30	SUNDAY SCHOOL, Morning	at 9-30
,, ,, Afternoon	at 2 0	,, ,, Afternoon	at 2-0

MASON'S KILLCORN — A marvellous and effective cure for Corns, Warts, etc. It acts like magic, giving immediate relief, completely killing the corn after a few applications. Sold by Chemists in 1/- bottles. Local Agents, TAYLORS' DRUG CO.

THE CLIFFORD HAIR RESTORER never fails to restore the Hair to its natural colour and gloss, preventing the hair from falling out, or coming off with the comb; removing Scurf and dandriff, and preserving the Scalp in a clean, cool, and healthy condition. 1/- each. Local Agents, TAYLORS' STORES.

DR. BUTLER'S TIC & TOOTHACHE CURE. One dose will quickly relieve the pain, while if repeated a few times a permanent cure will ensue. In Bottles, 1/1½ and 2/9. Agents: TAYLORS' DRUG STORES.

DR. MUNRO'S ASTHMA CURE. The Scientific Remedy by Inhalation for Asthma, Catarrh, Bronchitis, etc. Gives instant relief in Tins, 2/6 each. Local Agents, TAYLORS' DRUG CO. Limited.

A lovely lithograph, dated 1893, showing the Wesleyan Chapel. The sponsors offer cures for all ailments without divine help. Taylors merged with Timothy Whites and later with Boots the Chemists.

The first Catholic church and schoolroom situated in Barleyhill Road. The school was cleared each week for the service which was served by a priest from Aberford until 1964.

A new Catholic church was built in Station Road on land which had formerly been Green's Nurseries. It was never used for a service as it collapsed only days before it was due to be opened.

A procession believed to be carrying the cross from St Joseph's in Barleyhill Road to the new church.

The Catholic church in its collapsed state following rain and strong wind.

The church was rebuilt using the same architect, in a similar but stronger style. This was later deemed to be unsafe and was therefore demolished.

The current Catholic church, of different design but on the same site.

Four
Education

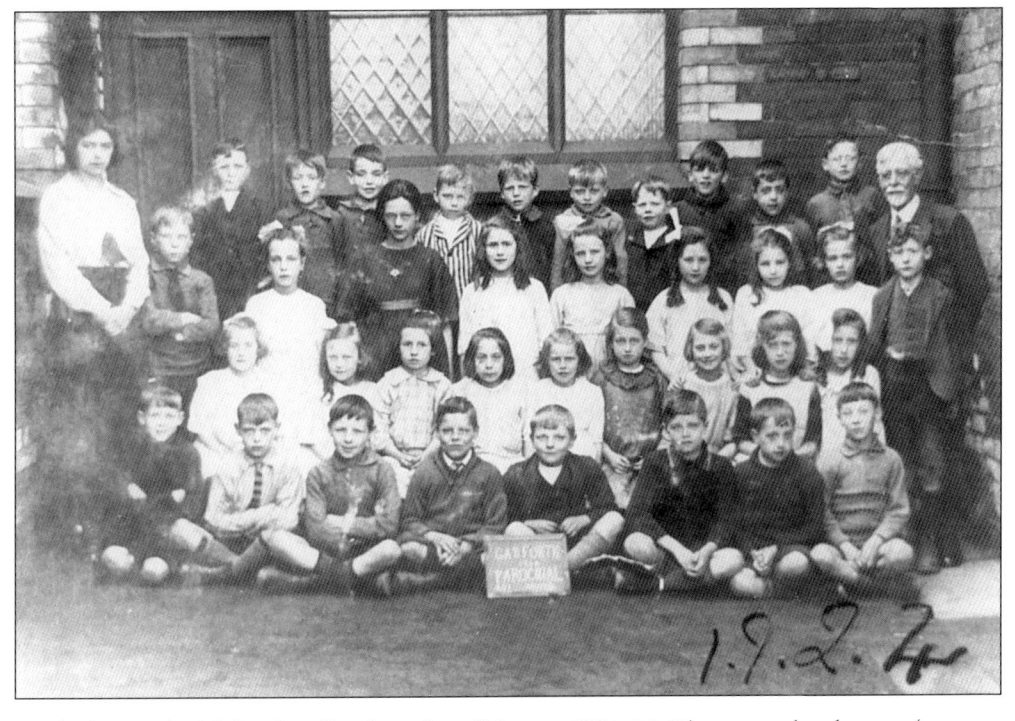

Garforth Parochial School staff and pupils in February 1924. Mr Thompson, headmaster (extreme right), retired that year, after almost thirty years' service, to be replaced by Mr Veitch.

GARFORTH PARISH SCHOOLS.

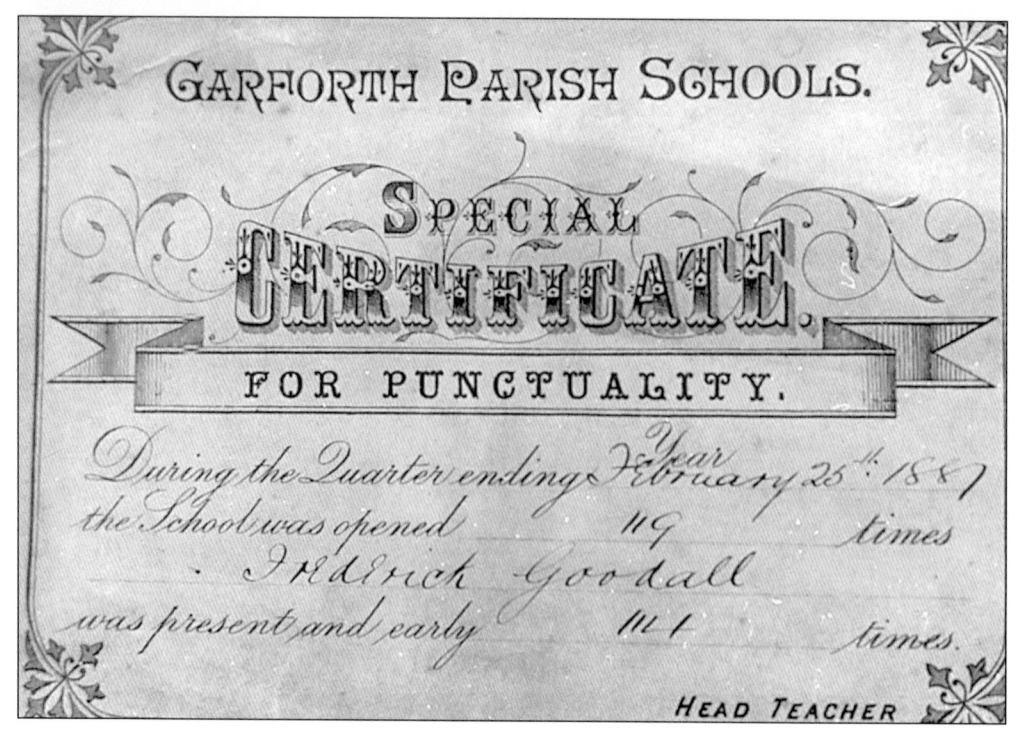

SPECIAL CERTIFICATE.

FOR PUNCTUALITY.

During the Quarter ending February 25th 1887 the School was opened 119 times. Frederick Goodall was present and early 114 times.

HEAD TEACHER

This was one way of encouraging attendance at school, which was not totally free until 1890. The teachers' salaries also depended on attendance, and attendance percentages figure prominently in the school log books of the time.

The Parochial School at the end of Church Lane in 1910.

The Parochial School football team, well kitted out and with medals displayed, also hold the Deighton Shield in 1911. Mr Thompson, headmaster, stands on the right at the back.

Pictured (left to right) are: Back row — Harry Balance, Ernest Turnpenny, Wilfred Warburton, Joseph Nicholson, Ernest Henshaw, Ray Watts; second row — Tommy Denton, Sid Limbert, Herbert Goodall, Jack Palmer, H. Goodall, H. Hancock, A. Holden, N. Knowles, J. Green; third row — William Below, Ernest Brownridge, George Dockerty, A. Gibbon, Wilfred Jackson, Dick Ward, Harry Barlow, B. Simpson; front row — Albert Lorryman, Arthur Dickinson, Norman Pratt, H. Wood, Bill Platts. Teachers in the group are Miss Flo James, Miss Simpson.

A newspaper cutting kept for many years by Harry Goodall. Flo James, the teacher on the left, well known later in village theatrical productions as Flo Toes, started as a monitor in 1921 on a salary of £26 per annum.

47

The Parochial School hockey team in 1927. Mr Veitch had been keen to organize sport and during the first few days of his headship had formed a school sports club and gained permission to use the ground of Garforth Athletic Football Club.

Mr Veitch formed a hockey team for the girls and within a month had also raised £10 for the sports fund by holding a dance and whist drive at St Mary's Hall.

Mr Rayson with the Parochial School's football team. He was headmaster between 1928 and 1947. The team won the Barkston Ash Cup in 1932, and are seen here with the Gascoigne Shield.

The Parochial School cricket team in 1933/34 with the headmaster, Mr Rayson. The players include Jim Nicholson and Harold Bramley.

A more recent photograph of the Parochial School in 1972. The trees have grown since the same, but earlier, view. Coke stoves were still used to heat the building.

The Medical Centre, built in 1994, on the site of the Parochial School. Builders found substantial remains of the air-raid shelter in the former school gardens, which were difficult to remove.

Girls at the Parochial School around 1931.

Pupils at St Joseph's Roman Catholic School, Barleyhill Road, in 1927. The photograph was lent by Mrs L. Ryder, *née* Kennedy, seen here on the knee of her older sister. She was only aged three, but was admitted to boost the school numbers and so prevent closure.

East Garforth School was built in 1843 by the Gascoigne family. It provided education for the children of their own colliers.

Just before the closure of East Garforth School the windows were decorated to celebrate its history. A new building was erected on adjacent land, this one becoming the Aagrah Restaurant.

Barleyhill Road School opened in 1907 amid controversy. Older Parochial schoolchildren's parents were told to send them to the new school, but the Parochial School Governors successfully opposed the move.

Taken around 1947, many of these children may still remember their time at Barleyhill Road School. Three at least, Penny Hollinrake, Pam Bean and Enid Haswell, returned for a time as teachers.

Mrs Gladys Gisburn donated this photograph of Barleyhill Road School in 1919. She is one of the children towards the right on the front row, while her husband Walter (Wally) is one of the boys hanging over the segregating fence.

During the Second World War Mrs Gisburn formed and ran a pre-school group for children of mothers engaged in war work.

Five
Main Street

This early view of an almost empty Main Street, then called Briggate, shows houses on both sides, though some had shops in their front rooms. The large building on the right is Eagle House, which stands at the end of Chapel Lane.

The pump at Town End, looking up Aberford Road with the Miners' Arms by the carts. Tom Pickering's house, with the tall roof apex, was pulled down to make the entrance to Oak Estate, Oak Road, around 1938.

Town End, with Wakefield Road ahead. We believe that the lady, hands on hips, is Mrs Hebden of Station Road. Squire Backhouse leans over the half door of his butcher's shop, across the corner, with Main Street off left.

The police station stood near the top of Main Street, now the site of Pease's car park, near the Co-op Stores. The force moved to new premises in Lidgett Lane in the 1970s.

An advertisement dated 1935, typical of many small businesses' publicity. One elderly lady, in 1977, reflects, 'We were a busy little place. Very self-sufficient.' The few telephones were connected to a manual exchange in a Lidgett Lane house.

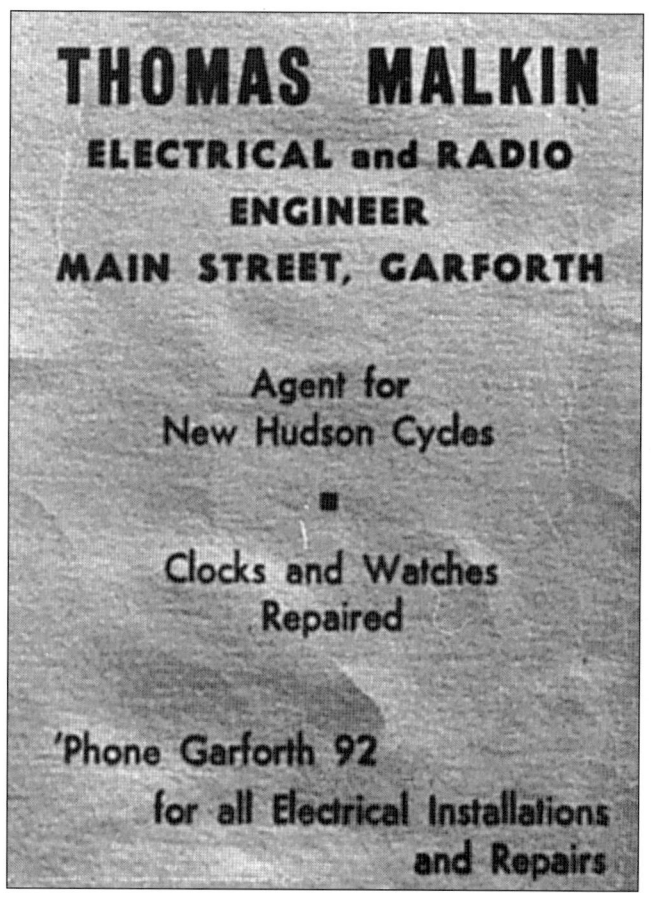

THOMAS MALKIN
ELECTRICAL and RADIO ENGINEER
MAIN STREET, GARFORTH

Agent for
New Hudson Cycles

■

Clocks and Watches
Repaired

'Phone Garforth 92
for all Electrical Installations
and Repairs

The top of Main Street around 1910. The boy is playing with a metal bowler, a hoop, which he would guide down the slope using a metal rod that had a hook on the end.

A recent view of the same shops. In the late nineteenth century this steeper part of Main Street was known as Catley Hill, named after a grocer who traded here before 1900, rather than the carpet shop.

Detail of the plaque on the previous picture. Newmarket Place was built by George Rex, also the builder of Kensington Terrace and the Newmarket Inn. We are reliably informed that he did not use winnings from Newmarket races to fund the building!

The keystone of the arch over Kensington Terrace. It has been suggested that the resemblance to a royal head may be a play on the name 'Rex'.

Mallison's shop, further down Main Street, also known as Reliance Stores. Mr Mallison toured the nearby villages, with a van selling groceries, in the early 1920s. 'For those to whom quality matters.'

Starkey's Shoe Repairers in Main Street in the 1950s. The building that housed Thorpe's newsagents is still standing but Starkey's was demolished and he moved his business into Barleyhill Road.

Although the photograph suggests that this is a house-shop, it had the grand name of George Mosby's Drapery Establishment, Central House. The Mosbys had several children one being Bright Mosby, mentioned in the Transport section.

CENTRAL HOUSE,
MOOR GARFORTH.
GEORGE MOSBY'S
Drapery Establishment
STOCKINGS KNITTED & FOOTED.

Men's and Boys' Hats. A New assortment of Ladies' Hats, Bonnets, Flowers, Feathers and Ribbons. Fancy Frillings, Laces and Fashionable Print.

DEALER IN
STEAD & SIMPSON'S BOOTS AND SHOES.

"I want a pair of Boots, Mr. Mosby; those I got of you have not worn too well, I have only had them about three years;" said Joseph Atkinson, of Micklefield.

Please come and buy, and we will try to satisfy you.

What questions this advertisement poses!

This fish and chip shop stood well back from the road on the east side of Main Street. Earlier still, it is believed to have been a shop and bakery run by Miss Barber, who supplied bread to the Gascoigne family.

The Chapel of Rest stands almost on the site of the shop in the previous picture.

In the same area stood 'Fatty' Fox's first cycle shop – 'Maker of Flying Fox Cycles'. He later became a baker with premises opposite Greensway. A Mr Shackleton took that business over and moved it to Church Lane.

A procession for the Festival Queen in the 1960s. Main Street still has houses. The West Riding Automobile Co. bus obscures Phillipson's cycle and electrical shop.

Freda Spencer, a fine baker, was well known for her cakes. The shop with the corner door, Balderson's shoe shop, is now the entrance to Tesco. Spencer's building still stands.

Taken by Mr Holroyd, the chemist, outside his first shop, the middle one in Newmarket Place. Has the snow proved too much for the Jowett Bradford? Mr Preston's barber's shop, and Miss Mary Preston's 'Hair Hut', are on the left.

The Welfare Hall, left, places the scene. Colliery Row and 'Long Curtain' Row have given way to a parade of shops. Jack Charlton, the footballer, once ran his men's wear business in one of them.

Mr and Mrs Ratcliffe took over Jordan's newsagents shop and it was run by Mrs Ratcliffe into the 1960s. The building is now used as offices by solicitors.

Helen Ratcliffe was photographed here when the shop still bore the name Jordan. She is standing at the entrance to what is now Greensway.

For many years this was *the* men's wear shop in Garforth. Harold Bramley is the youngster with the manager, Jack Haswell.

Many children got their sweets from 'Daddy Breckon's', now Fenwick Newsagents. Mr Breckon also kept the key for the water pump on the opposite side of the road.

Breckon's is the middle one of these three shops, built by Marshall builders. Breckon's shop provided an income for his three sons.

The shops viewed from the opposite direction. Louis Dimler, pork butcher, was said to be 'drummed out'. Possibly of German extraction, he was probably interned under the Defence of the Realm Act in the First World War.

Alfred Smith's was a grocery shop, later occupied by Mrs Holliday and then the Shaws. The premises now house the bookshop. The living quarters next door, Holly House, became the Leeds & Holbeck Building Society, and are now a fast food outlet.

Standing opposite Alfred Smith's on Barleyhill Road, was Preston's tailors seen here advertising Rover cycles. With the front rebuilt it became Knowles's greengrocers and is now Everett the butcher's.

T. B. SMITH,
General Supply Stores, GARFORTH.

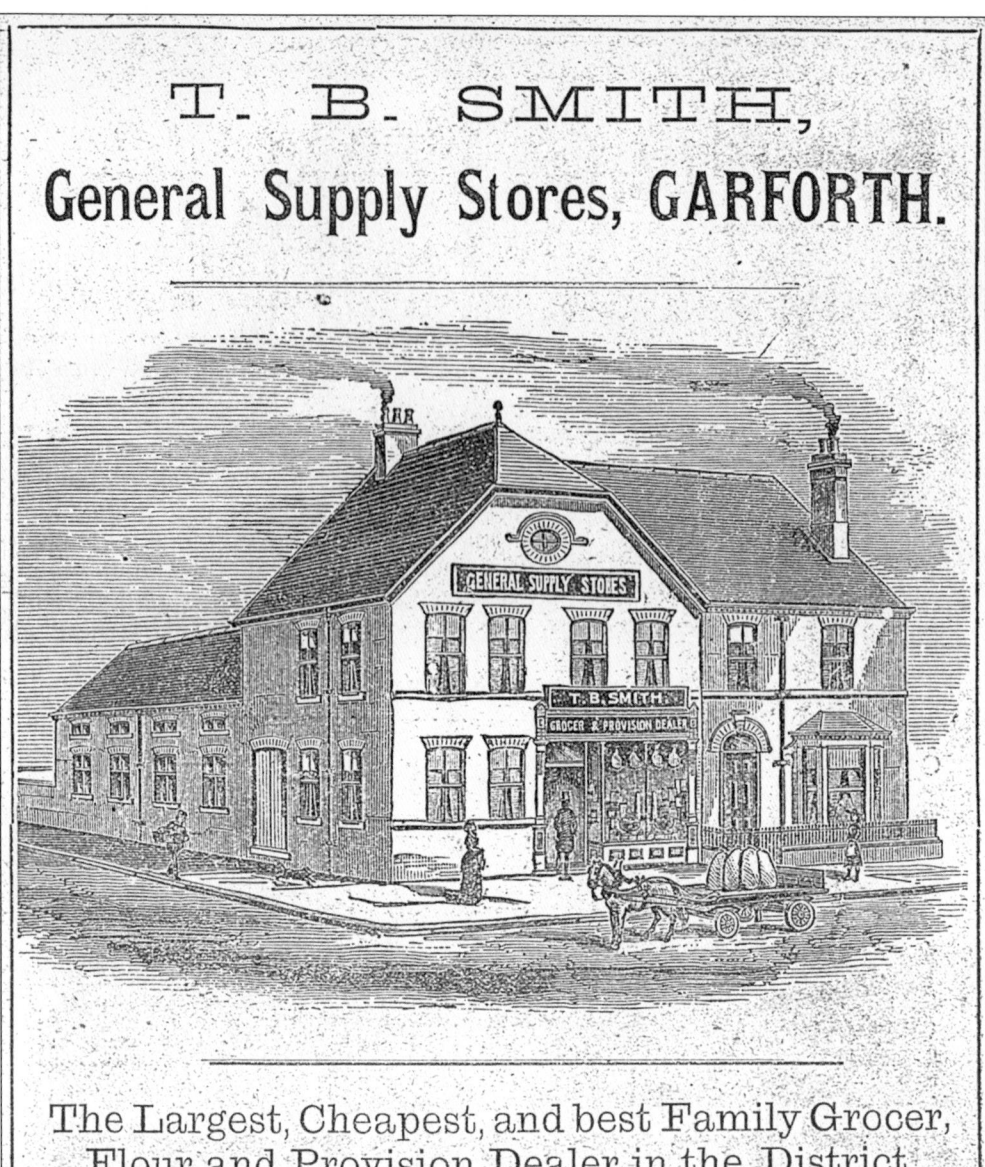

The Largest, Cheapest, and best Family Grocer, Flour and Provision Dealer in the District.

Our Excelsior Blends of Indian, China, and Ceylon Teas, are not surpassed for Purity, Strength and Flavour at 1/10, 2/4, and 3/- per lb.

Published by C. R. Massey, 35, Upperhead Row, Leeds.

A lithograph of T.B. Smith's shop which later became the offices of Garforth Urban District Council, until Garforth was swallowed up by Leeds.

The Council Offices. T.B. Smith's front was remodelled, but notice the oval window was carefully re-sited on the end wall. The frame on the roof held the air-raid siren.

A token issued by T.B. Smith's shop. Many stores issued such tokens. This one has a milled edge.

What a fine turnout! A young Flo Toes parked in Main Street just below Holly House. The private house is now the site of a café and take-away.

W. SECKER,
FAMILY GROCER, TEA DEALER,
AND PROVISION MERCHANT,
Holly House, GARFORTH.

Has on hand a large and varied stock of Groceries and Provisions, and all those who study economy would do well to call and inspect. The undermentioned are a few Specialities which he can recommend a with confidence.

	PER LB.	
FIRST CLASS FAMILY TEA	2s. 6d	HUNTLEY & PALMER, PEEK, FREAN & CO's. BISCUITS
VERY GOOD FAMILY TEA	2s. 0d	AGENT FOR LEWIS'S CELEBRATED BRITISH WINES
HAM RASHERS (from middle)	10d	
BACON RASHERS	7d	AGENT FOR BEAUFOY'S CELEBRATED BRITISH WINES
BACON in Pieces	6½d	
ANCHOR BRAND PURE ROLLER FLOUR— 1s. 8d. and 1s. 10d. per stone		AGENT FOR P. & P. CAMPBELL, PERTH DYE WORKS
BASS AND ALLSOPP'S INDIAN PALE ALE—		AGENT FOR S. MAY'S VEGETABLE AND FLOWER SEEDS
	½ pts. 2s. 4d	
Do. do. do.	Imp. pts. 4s. 3d	COPE'S, HIGNETT'S, AND OGDEN'S SUPERIOR TOBACCOS
GUINNESSES DUBLIN STOUT	½ pts. 2s. 0d	CHEQUE BANK CHEQUES FOR REMITTANCE
Do. do.	Imp. pts. 3s. 9d	TRY SECKER'S SUPERIOR BAKING POWDER

Parties in the outlying districts, called on fortnightly, and Goods delivered promptly.

EGGS, fine and fresh, 24 for a Shilling.

An 1884 advertisement for Holly House before it became Alfred Smith's. Prices are worth converting and comparing to present-day ones.

72

Six
Transport

The Manning Wardle-built *Empress*, at the Light Arch in Parlington, on the Fly Line from Garforth to Aberford.

The Leeds to Selby railway through Garforth was the first passenger line in Yorkshire. This drawing, created to show how the line might look as it passed over the Leeds to Selby turnpike at Halton Dial, has Halton Hill on the right and Killingbeck Hall on the left.

The first carriage used on the Fly Line. Before the use of engines it free-wheeled down the gradient to Aberford whilst a horse rode on a dandy-car. The horse then hauled the carriage back up to Garforth.

Hawks Nest cottage and the engine shed on the Fly Line to Aberford. The Hebden family, who lived in the cottage, are pictured here with the shunter, Bright Mosby, son of a grocer and draper with premises in Main Street.

The Manning Wardle engine *Empress* around 1921, taking children to the Roman Catholic school at Garforth. The estate workers seem to be on logging duties, judging by the crane.

Garforth Old Station, on the Parlington side of the railway bridge. The Gascoigne family could arrive, by coach, at the main line station from Parlington Hall by travelling along the 'Coach Road'.

Another view of the old station with the flight of steps behind. When visiting Safeway look for the steps which are still there, on the left side of the road bridge.

The present station, looking westward, with the old station through the bridge on the right-hand side.

A view of the station eastward from the road bridge. The footbridge connects the two platforms. The engine and trucks in the middle distance are joining the main line from the colliery Fly Line.

Station Road, but full of pigs not cars! There were three farms located here; these are Pickering's pigs off to market by rail.

Cows gathered where the station car park is now. Sisters pit is in the background.

The Garforth to Castleford railway crossed Ninelands Lane. The track is now a bridleway to Kippax. Mr Rickard's wagons from the sand workings joined the railway near this point.

This stone opposite Ninelands Lane end marks the turnpike road. On such roads users were charged tolls at 'bars' for the road's maintenance. Peckfield Bar stood on this road.

A postcard view from the railway bridge in Aberford Road showing farm buildings and Green's Nurseries, as well as the smart pony and trap on the 'wrong' side of the road.

The Pickering family being transported in earlier years.

Mr McHamish, as the advertisement says, ran a variety of means of transport from his garage at Town End. He also ran a 'miners' special' to Ledston Luck colliery.

'Any distance, any day' – but this may well have been determined by how long you could endure travelling with solid tyres.

J. McHAMISH & Co.

Pioneer Garage,

GARFORTH.

Char-a-Bancs and Taxis.

Pleasure Parties catered for.

ANY DISTANCE.   ANY DAY.

McHamish's taxis at his depot at Town End. This seems a remarkably large fleet for those days.

After the First World War, cyclecars were built as an alternative to motor-cycle and side car. This example belonged to Mr Oliver White who lived at West Garforth Farm. Gladys Maltby, née Stringer, is in the precarious dickey-seat.

Another early car, probably parked at the Gas Works down Barwick Road.

Tom Pickering's Hodgson car, one of only eight built at 25 Whitehall Road, Leeds. With a 1496cc Anzani engine and a four-speed Meadows gearbox, the touring model cost £395. The passenger is Mr C. Robinson.

Having had a motor-cycle and sidecar, Mary Preston's father, Harry, purchased this Calthorpe from Mr Sissons of Waterloo Manor for £45. In it they used to visit relatives at Helperby.

Mr Preston then acquired a Bullnose Morris, which type was produced until 1926. It stands in the yard behind his shop which was situated in Main Street opposite Newmarket Buildings.

Seven
People

Keen bowlers wearing flat caps.

Jabez Woolley was an early railway commuter between Garforth and Leeds where his family had a brickworks. He was a Methodist who involved himself in church matters. There is a window in memory of his son in Brunswick Chapel and an acknowledgement to his generosity in a chapel near Tockwith.

Jabez built this fine house, The Hollies, in Church Lane using his own bricks, of course. He was, with a neighbour, party to the building and re-alignment of Station Road (now Fields) on their own land, which is why it is still a private road today.

This brick was retained when the tram depot at Swinegate in Leeds was demolished.

Toll Bar House where tolls were collected when Aberford Road was a turnpike. The last toll-keepers were the Dixon family and pictured left to right are Alfred Dixon, an unknown lady, Sam, Edgar and Lucy Hodgkinson, an unknown child, Mrs Dixon and Helen Dennison.

Mr and Mrs J.H. Pickering. He was a farmer and founder of the retail and wholesale butchering business later taken over by his son, Tom.

88

The Revd Wilford who followed his father in the inter-war years as Rector at Garforth. He had considerable land and property in Garforth and was known to leave 2s 6d on the mantelpiece when visiting parishioners who were not well.

The King George V Silver Jubilee Committee. The Revd Wilford gave the land opposite Barleyhill Road school for the creation of the Recreation Ground.

Mrs Margaret Eleanor Whitwell, the first lady councillor on Garforth Urban District Council. These were the days when local decisions were made by local people.

A member of the Mosby family who were miners, but were also heavily involved in local Methodist preaching.

Although Leeds-born, Sgt Albert Mountain, VC, Croix de Guerre, Médaille Militaire, was the publican at the Miners' Arms. His Victoria Cross was for extreme valour in 1918, and here he is being honoured by his old school.

Mr J.E. Gray (in uniform extreme right) and members of his family. The man in the trilby, seated centre and nursing a little girl, is Mr Jim Breckon the shopkeeper.

After the Armistice in 1918, this Peace Celebration was held in June 1919 on land between Beech Grove Avenue and Terrace. C.L. Sharpe, the curate, stands in the centre of the picture and Mrs Goodall, of Strawberry Avenue, is one of the children at the front.

This celebration was held by the Beech Grove residents, on 21 September 1945, following the end of the war with Germany in May and Japan in August that year.

The residents of the Oak Estate celebrate the Queen's Coronation in 1953. Many people will recognize themselves and remember that day.

The 1935 Jubilee Queen and her attendants, from left to right: Sydney Waters, Kingsley Brownridge, Muriel Griffin, Margaret Simpson, Winnie Stead (Queen), Beryl Freeman, Peter Kimberley, Mona Bellhouse, Bob Walker.

Another Garforth resident to achieve fame was Air Chief Marshal 'Gus' Walker, DSO, DFC, who lost an arm attempting to rescue the crew of a burning plane. He lived in the big house at the corner of Lidgett Lane and Lowther Road.

A wedding reception held by the Malkin family at East Garforth School. In earlier times East Garforth was a separate community with its own football team and a Church Mission at the top of Newhold.

Eight
Buildings

Garforth Old Hall stood almost opposite the Gaping Goose pub. Although Elizabethan it was demolished for the proposed dual carriageway which was never built. It was once the centre of West Garforth; it is supposed that people moved away and rebuilt the village elsewhere after an outbreak of plague.

OLD BARROWBY.   [Jone

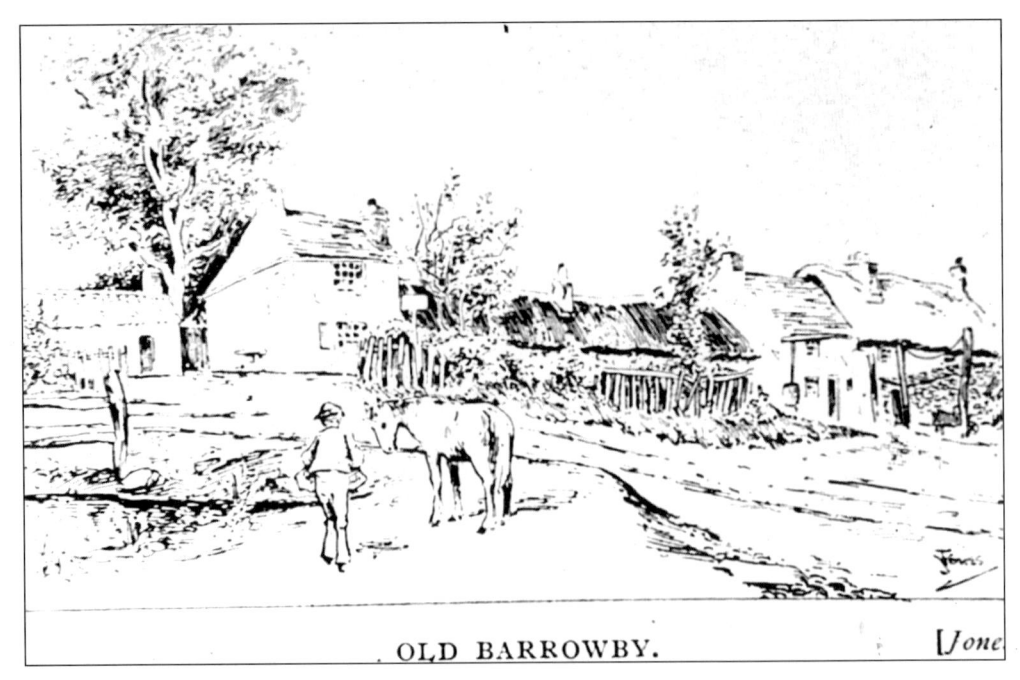

Edmund Bogg, a Leeds bookseller and amateur historian, published several books on old Yorkshire. This drawing from one shows cottages, now demolished, beyond the level crossing on Barrowby Lane. Humps and hollows now show where they once stood.

One of the above, Mrs Tillotson's farm cottage was nearest to Barrowby Lane, and from it she sold milk and eggs to Garforth residents until 1929.

Another of this group of cottages, said to be one of the first meeting places for Garforth Methodists, although the properties are, strictly speaking, in the parish of Barwick in Elmet.

During demolition of the cottages Mr George Smith photographed the 'cruck' construction, rare in this area. This image was rescued after Mr Smith's death by Mr Walter Pickles.

Parlington Hall, *c.* 1880, with its conservatory or maybe an orangery, which was fashionable at that time. Lords of the Manor, the Gascoignes lived here prior to moving to Lotherton.

Beatrice Selby, later Mrs Ward, lived in Gardener's Cottage in Parlington around 1930. She and her friends are standing on the footbridge over the Fly Line between the Dark Arch and the deer park.

A later, postcard, view bearing a George V halfpenny stamp. The sender says, 'This is a view of the house they are letting go to ruin.' It was demolished in the 1950s.

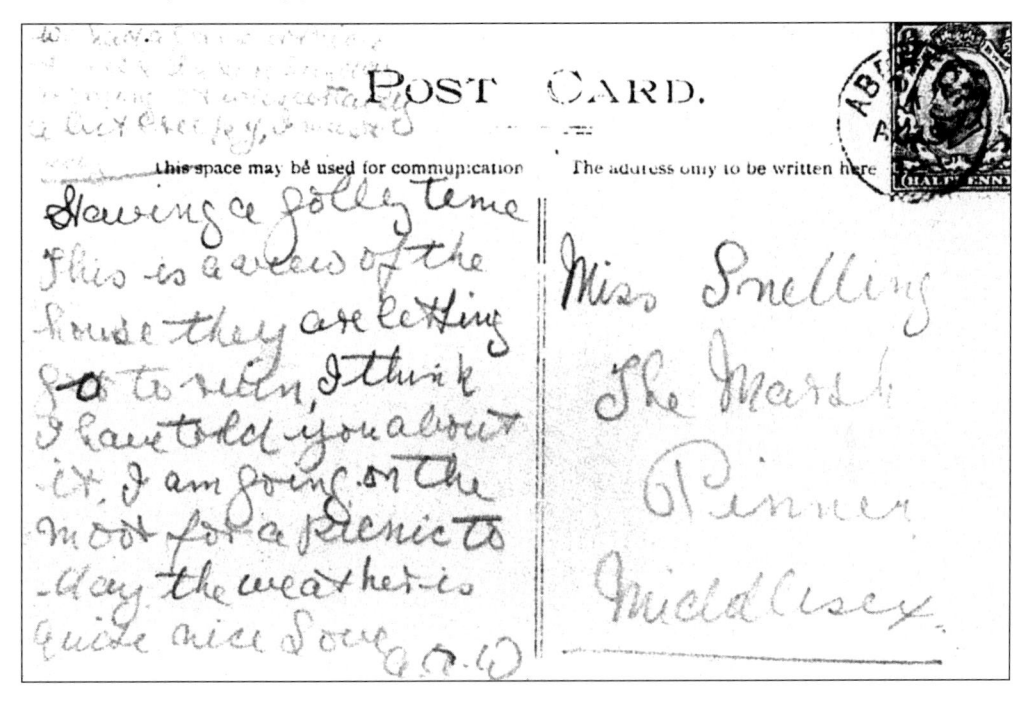

Col. Frederick Trench-Gascoigne, who succeeded to the Parlington estate in 1905, found it damp and moved to Lotherton. This his son Sir Alvary gave to Leeds Corporation in 1968, two years before his death.

For landowners, lakes were status symbols. The Gascoignes had two made by damming the Cock Beck. This one was later drained because it was feared it might flood the pit workings.

Tom Pickering's house photographed from the back garden. It was demolished around 1938 to make access to the new Oak Estate from Aberford Road.

A garden party in front of the old Rectory, c. 1919. The Rectory was demolished in 1972 and is now the site of Croft Foulds Court.

Rose Villa. This fine, large house stood back from Church Lane. Its grounds are now the site of Rose Court.

The Grange was originally the curate's house, then the home of Miss Merry, who ran a nursery school. The house was demolished to make access to Grange Estate, which takes its name from its predecessor.

Brookfield, on Selby Road, Garforth, was the home of Mr John Clapham Bartle. He was a notable land auctioneer and estate agent who owned the cattle market behind the Brown Cow public house at Whitkirk.

Leylands on Selby Road, well known for NSPCC garden parties, was formerly Hawkshaw House. Once owned by T.B. Smith, whose shop we have featured, it had been a private boarding school for boys as shown in the 1871 Census.

De Grey House stands on Wakefield Road near the junction with Main Street. Other homes have been built where this garden once flourished.

This postcard shows the front of De Grey House. The houses lower down Wakefield Road are still recognizable today. The state of the road and the absence of traffic are the real changes.

Sturton Lane, East Garforth, was earlier known as Paradise (spelled incorrectly on the postcard). These houses still remain.

The houses on the right are still clearly recognizable in Sturton Lane although nowadays traffic to new estates preclude standing in the street.

The earlier Old George at Garforth Bridge was a coaching inn with stables at the rear. This photograph was taken before 1920, as there is no garage yet on the opposite corner. The Sheffield (Sheep field) Beck, which runs under the road at this point, was the parish boundary.

St Mary's Hall, Church Lane, built on the stackyard used for the farming activities at the Rectory. It was used by many groups and societies until it was burned in a fire and finally demolished, along with the Scout and Guide huts, to be replaced by houses.

The Gascoigne Arms around 1960, now known as Gascoignes. The pub, located in Station Road, sold Bentley's Yorkshire Beer which was brewed at Woodlesford.

A faded, early view of the Miners' Arms at Town End, where Albert Mountain VC was once landlord. It was previously the Jolly Collier, or locally named 'Vince's' after another landlord. Earlier still it is recorded as the Black Bull.

The Gaping Goose inn on Selby Road appropriately with Mr Billy Previll and geese in the foreground. Believed to be the oldest public house in Garforth, serving travellers on this former turnpike road, and the folk of West Garforth.

The Gaping Goose in the 1930s when it sold Melbourne Ales, brewed in Regent Street at Leeds. The roof of the old Elizabethan hall (shown earlier) can be seen on the right.

Dar Villas cottages before they were rebuilt as bungalows. Continued resurfacing had raised the road level much higher than the pavement. A Mr Westerman recalls stones hitting the windows as they were thrown up by passing traffic.

Seaton's house and stable on Station Road. This family of coal merchants only ever used horse transport. Although these buildings have since been demolished, the replacement office block retains the name 'Seaton House'.

Garforth Picture House stood back from Station Road at Town End, between the garage and the Miners' Arms. The programme changed twice each week with a matinée for children on Saturday.

The cinema site is now that of Pease's who moved here after occupying the old Co-op premises in Main Street. Their car park was once the site of the old police station.

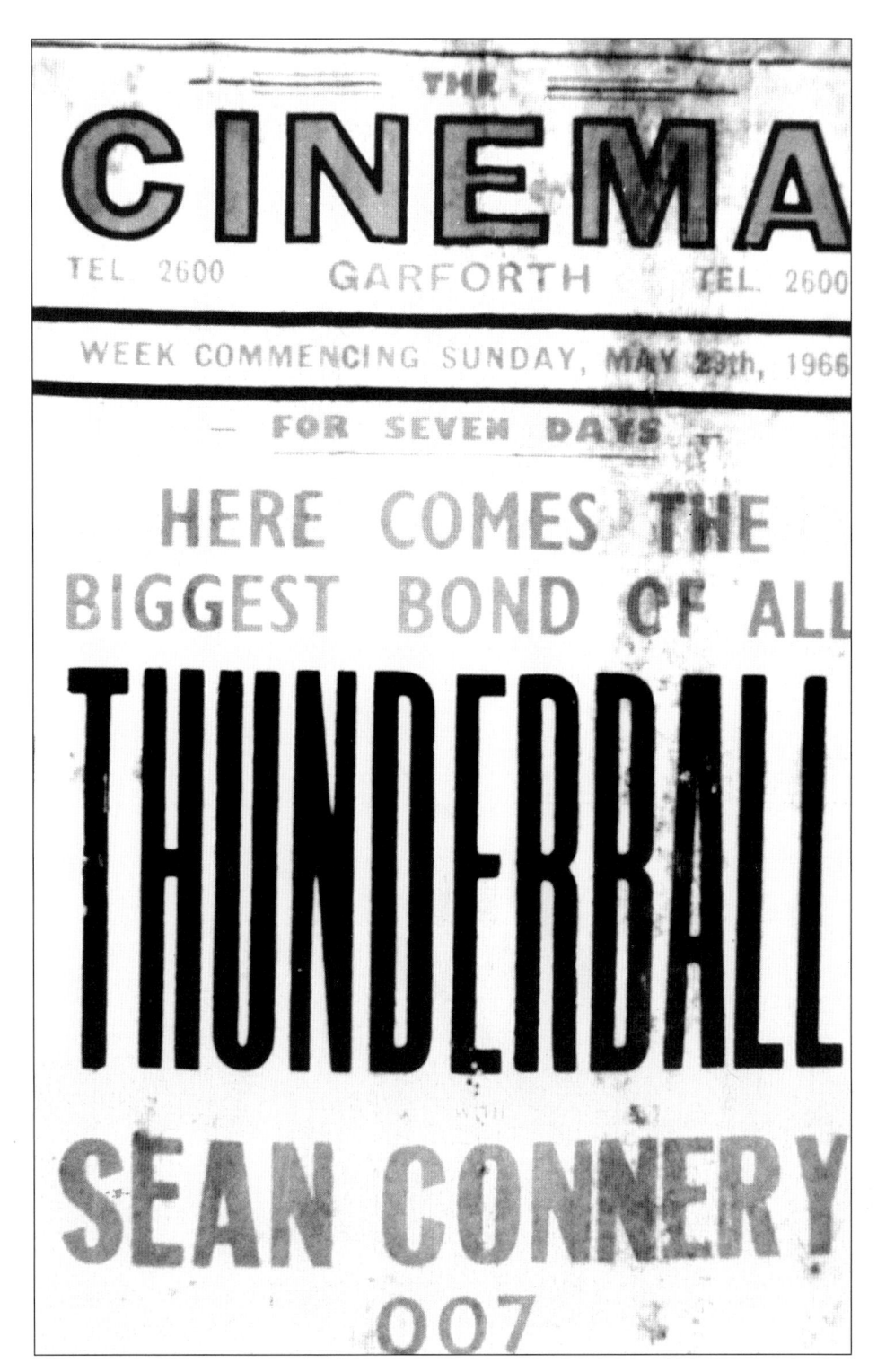

Donated by Mrs Stocks, of Oak Road, this May 1966 poster shows the very popular Bond film was held for seven days rather than the usual three.

These buildings stood in Church Lane at the junction with Lidgett Lane, on the site of today's library. They included Varley's hairdressers, Laycock's newsagents and Shackleton's bakery.

To the left is Springfield House in Lowther Road, with Lowther Avenue to the right. Once it was the home and surgery of Dr Sidney Griesbach and his large family; it was later owned and used by Dr J.F. Robinson. These buildings now form Springfield Residential Home.

Nine
Leisure

The following pages illustrate how people made their own entertainment. Garforth Brass Band in 1890 consisted of, from left to right, back row: W. Cockrem, Bob Limbert, Billy Limbert, Joe Learoyd, Charles Cockrem, W. Gedge, W. Bennett, Harry Pease, Joseph Vince. Middle row: Alfred Collins, Alfred Dixon, David Howcroft, Harry Oxtoby, Aaron Howson, George Dixon, A. Hudson, Seth Hudson. Front row: Ned Goodall, William Booth.

A carnival on Aberford Road in Edwardian times. The ladies looking over the railings are in Salisbury Terrace.

Another carnival view of around the same time showing the cottage which housed the Yorkshire Penny Bank (hence 'Bank Row'), Seaton's house and, on the right, the Miners' Arms and Tom Pickering's substantial house.

Fun to be had with the Garforth Comic Band who are also advertising a Whist Drive. Kippax also had a Comic Band and one wonders how keen the competition was between them.

Garforth Brass Band, of a slightly later period, with a recurrence of many familiar local names including Backhouse, Wilson, Roberts, Learoyd, Pratt, Westerman, Brownridge and Holden.

Sports being held on fields in front of the houses named Sisters Villas, off Barwick Road. The slag heap of the Sisters pit is in the background.

A garden party held at the Rectory. Mrs Winnie Gaythorpe and her mother are both in the group.

An early group of local Boy Scouts.

East Garforth, often regarded as a separate village, had its own football team. Players in 1912/13 included Mr Bailey-Hartford, A. Mathews, T. Jones, S. Smith, Capt. Attwell, L. Holden, R. Brownridge, F. Wilson, T. Howson, A. Howson, H. Malkin, G. Dacre.

Garforth Villa Football Team, in 1924, at Garforth Working Men's Club. Members include W. Browning, Mr Hudson (trainer), R. Kilburn, H. Siberry, J. Birch, Mr Cockram, W. Burnett, J. Dobson. A. Limbert, J. Hill, S. Shillito, G. Prince, T. Watts, B. Hamilton.

A more recent Garforth bowling team. From left to right: B. Hullan, A. Gill, H. Craven, M. Hitchcock, C. Holmes, A. Cockram, D. Atack (with cup), H. Hancock, K. Tiffany, J. Brownridge and, seated in front, Harold 'Cocky' Howson.

Ten
General Views

An aerial view of Garforth in 1924, courtesy of Leeds City Libraries. Main Street is clearly seen running diagonally from top left to bottom right. Town End, Marshall's brickworks, with chimney, and the Welfare Hall can be easily identified.

A more elevated view of Station Fields from the Aberford Road railway bridge, looking towards the church, over what is now the Oak Estate. Barbers had the farm on the corner during the 1914-18 period.

Church Lane and St Mary's Church from the Bar Lane railway bridge before Oak Estate was built. Foreground ridges remain from the old field system before the Enclosure Act.

The cottages in Bank Row at Town End. The Yorkshire Penny Bank used the front room of the cottage on the right on a regular basis.

Town End and Aberford Road before cars. The owner of the cart on the right sold ice cream in summer and hot peas in the winter. The Miners' Arms is on the right.

121

The top of Church Lane close to where Oak Crescent now starts. The cottages on the left were demolished. The tree on the right marks where St Mary's Hall later stood.

Church Lane from the end of Oak Crescent. Atkinson's Farm, on the left of the cottages, is now the site of the Podger pub. Its name came from the special tool used at nearby Archibald Johnson's engineering works.

A 1930s postcard view of Church Lane and St Mary's Church behind the trees.

Although the postcard says Church Street it shows the junction of Church Lane with Main Street. On the left is the Parochial School. The message on the reverse suggests that it was being sent home by a dairy maid at the Manor Farm College.

Older residents referred to Barleyhill Road as 'the Occy' and the caption on this postcard explains why. In one nineteenth-century census it is Barleyhill Road as far as Providence Place and then Occupation Lane for the rest of the way.

Beech Grove Avenue before the street was surfaced, and before the iron railings were removed during the Second World War. Children play happily in the road with not a car in sight.

Ninelands Lane, unsurfaced, with Trench pit and Garforth Cliff in the distance. The fence on the right encloses what later became the cemetery.

Unmade Aberford Road at the junction with Bar Lane. Toll Bar cottage stands on the left and X marks the Colliery School. Green's Nurseries grew their trees and shrubs in the gated field on the right and 'Paradise' is beyond.

A 1919 postcard showing a post-war posed group from the Searchlight Unit. This was based where the Firthfields Community Centre is now located. The houses in the background on Sturton Lane confirm the site.

A Second World War gun site at East Garforth, photographed in 1980. New housing, Cedar Ridge, was built here in 1998 and excavations revealed a Romano-British site.

Viewed from Cramby Hill on Wakefield Road we see Selby Road with the Old George and Fitton's Garage (left) rising to the Gaping Goose (centre). Bowman's Well Green Farm, later Lindley's (right) is now the site of the Hilton Hotel.

The view from Sisters Villas across the fields, with the Coach Road and Manor Farm at the top left-hand corner. The medieval field system can be clearly seen.

These parallel lines of wooden-post holes, on the site where Cedar Ridge is built, indicate a huge barn-like structure of Romano-British times. A coin of Emperor Commodius (AD 180) was found here.

Part of a Romano-British 'Grubenhouse', a semi-sunken circular dwelling with low wattle walls above ground, at the Cedar Ridge site. A centre post supported a thatch type of roof. A stone quern for grinding corn was also found at the same site.